Wolf Sanctuary

The Wolves of Speedwell Forge

Schiffer Publishing Ltd®

4880 Lower Valley Road • Atglen, PA 19310

Chuck Rineer

Designed by RoS
Cover design by Brenda McCallum

Type set in Adobe Garamond Pro/Chaparral Pro

ISBN: 978-0-7643-5490-8
Printed in China

Published by Schiffer Publishing, Ltd.
4880 Lower Valley Road
Atglen, PA 19310
Phone: (610) 593-1777; Fax: (610) 593-2002
E-mail: Info@schifferbooks.com
Web: www.schifferbooks.com

For our complete selection of fine books on this and related subjects, please visit our website at www.schifferbooks.com. You may also write for a free catalog.

Schiffer Publishing's titles are available at special discounts for bulk purchases for sales promotions or premiums. Special editions, including personalized covers, corporate imprints, and excerpts, can be created in large quantities for special needs. For more information, contact the publisher.

We are always looking for people to write books on new and related subjects. If you have an idea for a book, please contact us at proposals@schifferbooks.com.

Other Schiffer Books on Related Subjects:
Animals Impacting the World. Dinah Roseberry & Mary Gasparo
ISBN: 978-0-7643-4237-0

Contemporary Wildlife Art. Cindy Ann Coldiron
ISBN: 978-0-7643-4864-8

Inside a Bald Eagle's Nest: A Photographic Journey through the American Bald Eagle Nesting Season. Teena Ruark Gorrow & Craig A. Koppie
ISBN: 978-0-7643-4464-0

This book is dedicated to the memory of Bill Darlington,
who introduced me to his wolves in the late 1970s. Also to Barbara, Bill's wife and
co-founder of the sanctuary; their daughter Dawn, president of Wolf Sanctuary of PA;
Darin Tomkins, the on-site caretaker of the wolves;
and all of the volunteers who dedicate their time and talents to the survival
of the wolves of Speedwell Forge.

"I have been fortunate to be a recipient of some of Chuck's amazing work. Through his eyes, I see the story of the lives of the wolves. It's Chuck's work that shows me their joy, their closeness, their love of life, and their ferocious beauty. He captures the unique and individual personality of every one of the Wolves of Speedwell."

—Stacey Youcis
Local hospital administrator and neighbor to the
Wolves of Speedwell

"Incredible and amazing: the words to describe the awesome photography of Chuck Rineer. His ability to capture the intense, yet calming look of these beauties is just amazing. Chuck knows when that perfect moment is to take a photo that will keep a memory forever. I am in awe of his artistic eye in photography."

—Denise Moyer-Lehman
State of the Art Design

After spending just shy of three decades in the military, **CHUCK RINEER** decided to rekindle his high school hobby of photography. He decided early on that he would concentrate on wildlife and nature. Finding himself drawn to Wolf Sanctuary of PA, he signed up as a volunteer photographer. Since 2007, he has been photographing these magnificent creatures, learning all he could as the years passed.

Chuck feels fortunate to have his photos used in numerous publications, including *The Washington Post*, *National Geographic Magazine's* online photo library, many periodicals, books, photo gallery events, and artist's renditions as well. He is fascinated whenever he looks through his camera lens at what wildlife has to offer and how much we can learn from it.

"Chuck continues to catch the wandering essence of the majestic wolf in his instinctual photographic moments. It's a true gift to capture the spirit of such a powerful and beautiful animal. Chuck is a master at showing us the emotional intensity, richness of colors, and amazing textures permeating the wolves at Speedwell. He celebrates his love of nature in every photograph. I am absolutely absorbed into each of his compositions."

—E. J. Moate
Art Education Millersville University

Contents

Foreword

by Dawn Darlington

I have known Chuck Rineer for nine years, but his first introduction to the sanctuary came long before that. He has volunteered his time and talent here at Wolf Sanctuary of PA since 2007. He came to me in April 2016 and told me he was working on a picture book of the Wolves of Speedwell. He asked if I would write the foreward, and I was more than happy to do so, but unsure of how to begin . . .

As we look to the future, we remember the past. William Henry (Bill) Darlington is my dad and Barbara Darlington is my mom. Together they did great things. With the passing of my papa Jerry, dad's father, the days of operating a dairy were done. Dad had always believed that you must follow your passion or be consumed by the passé. If you could not follow your passion, be passionate about what you do. Dad was passionate about mom, plants, and animals. Wolves had always been dad's passion and occupied a large part of his heart. In 1976, he was given a wolfdog, and in 1980 the laws in Pennsylvania changed regarding exotic animals. Wolves and wolfdogs were classified as exotics, and if you owned an exotic animal you had to apply for a special permit through the Pennsylvania State Game Commission. My parents applied for and were granted a menagerie permit to keep their wolf and wolfdog. I suppose the story could have ended there, but it didn't. The game commission asked my dad if, rather than euthanize every wolf they find, could they bring them to live under the Darlington's permit? My father was thrilled to accept.

That was 1980. It was also when my dad and Chuck first met. Chuck is retired military and so was dad. They met while volunteering at the YMCA's annual triathlon. The route happened to pass our property. They connected and found common ground in their military background, but soon discovered their commonality did not end there. They loved their families deeply, respected and were loyal to their nation, and valued our national treasures. Of course, to them our national treasures, among other things, encompassed the air we breathe, the land we walk on, and the animals that share our planet.

"Have you ever met a wolf pup?" Dad invited Chuck and his family to come meet his wolves. Wolves you say! Intrigued and excited, Chuck did visit with his family. They spent several hours together meeting the Wolves of Speedwell, and then went home. Life happened. In 1993, Dad incorporated as a 501c3 but was already feeling the strain on his body from the cancer that would later steal him from our side. He passed from lymphoma in 1998. Mom continued on the path they had started together—to offer a safe haven to wolves and wolf dogs—but remained private. She missed her soulmate and would stay withdrawn for several years.

I moved home in 2005. When I moved home it was twofold. I needed to be here for Mom (although I feared we were way too much alike) and to restore my grandparents' home, a 1760s-ironmaster's mansion. It was my intent to share the home with visitors as a bed and breakfast of Speedwell Forge; it was never my intent to operate the Wolf Sanctuary. But as the work ended on the B&B, I found myself being drawn to the wolves and wolfdogs.

I started to wonder why no one visited to learn about the wolves. There was much to be done. The sanctuary was languishing.

I had a new direction in mind and went to Mom to ask for her opinion and her blessing. She was worried and unsure. Tours? Education? Would people come? Dad would have been excited. She gave me the green light and transferred the presidency of the sanctuary to me at the end of 2007.

That same year Chuck came back to visit. I was still very much behind the scenes. Chuck completed a volunteer waiver and offered to help. We started educational tours, small at first and only on weekends. Chuck and Denny (now our volunteer manager) became tour guides with no training. Just their passion. Chuck asked if he could take a few photos. He had just gotten this cool new camera. He would sit in the few enclosures we had for hours with the caretaker. Sometimes he would sit alone or with another volunteer. He did beautiful work from the beginning, documenting the wolves and wolf dogs that lived here. He captured precious moments as pups were born and grew up.

The years slid by. I became more active in the sanctuary. As we grew, rules were established, and the educational tours were improved and refined. What started out as a few visitors dropping by on their way in to town blossomed into groups of adults and children visiting for scheduled educational tours. Chuck continued as a tour guide, but he also started printing his work and donated many prints to sell to help care for the wolves. He came up with beautiful portraits of many pack members, and through his photographs he has preserved memories that will stretch past our time.

The path from there to here has been a whirlwind of emotions and learning and enlightenment. The sanctuary is not an "I" so much as a "we." There are amazing individuals who make up the team that has come together to represent Wolf Sanctuary of PA. The volunteers and the staff are all exemplary in their passion to educate and care for our rescues and to share of themselves with the visitors of the sanctuary. My dad would have been so proud to have stood by Chuck's side to talk about all the faces represented in this book: The souls that have come and gone and just how and what we can all do to protect our nation's treasures.

We will continue to work to provide a home that is as close as possible to a natural environment for wolves and wolf dogs for as long as we have the support to do so. By your capable hands and compassion do we continue in our mission. Thank you, Chuck, for sharing your amazing photos, to Mom and Dad for their love and understanding in a time when few knew or cared, to the volunteers that give freely their time, and to all those that visit every tour day.

Dawn Darlington

Born February 1966, Dawn grew up on a dairy farm, the same farm that would later become Wolf Sanctuary of PA. Dawn's childhood was happy and full of love and hard work. She was raised to appreciate the earth and the resources that come from it and to look evenly to the future and to the past. She is happiest outside, but finds that inside tasks tend to fill most of her time. Dawn's education started at birth with plants and animals, chess games, long walks with her mom, and tractor rides with her dad. She graduated from Warwick High School and completed graphic arts training at Brownstown Vo-Tech during high school. She received an Associates of Science in electronics at DeVry University. Fifteen weeks prior to graduation, she was hired by Hughes Aircraft and moved to Los Angeles, California, after graduation. By day, she worked as an electronics technician, and at night attended college taking law classes and continuing education. Dawn eventually graduated from the University of West Los Angeles School of Law with a Bachelor of Science and holds certificates in corporate law and probate law. She is and always has been a determined individual. Dawn has been president of Wolf Sanctuary of PA since 2007 and owner/operator of Speedwell Forge B&B and the real estate since 2006.

Preface

This book represents a small number of photos that I've taken from 2007 through 2017 of some of the most fascinating creatures I've ever had the opportunity to photograph. I've chosen photos that inspired me to learn more and hope it will do the same for you.

Acknowledgments

To Dawn and her mother, Barbara: Thank you just doesn't seem like enough, but it's the best way I can express my gratitude for allowing me to photograph these amazing creatures that Bill Darlington called "The Wolves of Speedwell." A special thank you to Darin Tomkins for the countless hours that he affords me out of his unimaginable schedule when I have a particular need for a photo and for sharing his knowledge with me to better understand the wolves.

An unmeasurable thank you is in order for my great friend, Denny Binkley. A fair number of my photos would not have become reality without Denny's due diligence in watching out for an all-too-curious wolf. He familiarized himself with every possible exhibition of body language Lucas would use to warn of an impending try for my camera lens. The word "lunge" became a term in our vocabulary used regularly while photographing the wolves.

Most importantly, my endeavor would not be possible without the support of my lifelong partner, best friend, and toughest critic, my wife, Pam.

CHAPTER 1

For more than thirty years the Darlington family has offered refuge to wolves who have found themselves without a place in the natural world. It has been over a hundred years since the last wild wolf was known to exist in Pennsylvania. Originally created as a private rescue, Wolf Sanctuary of PA has grown into an educational facility. The Wolves of Speedwell hold a unique position as ambassadors to the wild. It has been said that "the best wolf habitat resides in the human heart." Perhaps it is also that the best habitat for our own wildness resides in the heart of the wolf. The sanctuary currently provides food, shelter, and veterinary care for over forty wolves with no government funding. It's only through the continued public support and interest that the Wolves of Speedwell thrive.

Wolf Sanctuary of PA

and Its Staff

Dawn Darlington (right) serves as the president of Wolf Sanctuary of PA, and Darin Tomkins (left) is the onsite care taker. They both know the pleasures and the challenges of operating the sanctuary on a daily basis.

I first met Barbara, co-founder of the Sanctuary, in 1978, when Bill invited me and my then three-year-old son, Jason, to visit their home to see "something special." Barbara had a fish pond that was full of goldfish and frogs. My son, now in his forties, remembers Barbara scolding, "Don't fall in the pond!" and "Leave my frogs alone!" Barbara and I still laugh about it today as does Jason. The "something special" that Bill wanted to show us was their first two wolf pups. Barbara is still a great friend and one that I hold dear to my heart. That day was the start of it all.

Denny Binkley has become a great friend to me and my photography over the years. I refer to him as my spotter as he watches my back while photographing the wolves. Denny is also the volunteer manager responsible for assigning tasks to the volunteers on tour days.

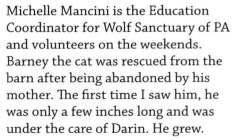

Michelle Mancini is the Education Coordinator for Wolf Sanctuary of PA and volunteers on the weekends. Barney the cat was rescued from the barn after being abandoned by his mother. The first time I saw him, he was only a few inches long and was under the care of Darin. He grew.

While there is no possible way to get all of the volunteers of Wolf Sanctuary of PA together at one time, I wanted to include a photo of some of the dedicated staff. Their continued support of my photography is greatly appreciated.

CHAPTER 2

There have been several dens dug since I started taking photographs at the sanctuary. Trinity as the alpha female in the Big Pack, the largest wolf pack at the Sanctuary, engineered two dens that would be used for having pups, which is the purpose of the wolf den. There was another den started in the rock pile located at the lower front of the Big Pack. I went inside the upper den, and Darin went in the one further down the hill just to check them out. Darin, during his expedition, estimated that the tunnel leading to the chamber where the pups would be born was at least ten feet down. The rock pile den didn't look safe from the beginning. Denny and I investigated and found the rocks to be unsafe and ready to cave in. It eventually did. There are times when you can still find a wolf disappearing down the entrance to hide a bone or deer hide.

The Wolf Den

The photo above is the entrance to one of the dens for the Big Pack. The tunnel is large enough for me to crawl down, but I had to back out.

From my observations, the alpha female is primarily responsible for the den.
After all, it's where she will birth her pups—a nursery of sorts.
Pictured on the right is the entrance to the second den in the Big Pack's territory.

Usually, the alpha female is responsible for den construction. This particular day, Tioga the omega male, the low wolf in a pack, decided to test his digging skills. We thought it possible that Tioga felt that since a female in the pack, Keisha, was tempting him to mate, he should help dig the den. In he went and the dirt was flying. When Keisha realized what he was doing, she came to the den entrance and displayed her displeasure with him by chasing him into the spring behind the den. Tioga walked into the middle of the spring seeking safe haven. He found out quickly, though, that Keisha could still grab his tail and pull him out of the water. He turned and headed up the hill and right back into the den. Before he could get his entire large body down inside, she grabbed a mouth full of his rump and dragged him out of the entrance. The entire time, Merlin, the alpha male and Tioga's father, stood back as if he knew not to tamper with her den. Once Keisha took back control of the construction, Merlin and Tioga couldn't do anything but stand above the entrance and watch the expert put her den in order. Denny and I agreed that this day was one of the best experiences of our time at the sanctuary and one that will be tough to beat.

Tioga stands in the pond, while Keisha grabs him by the tail.
Then Tioga takes a break from digging, and Keisha lets him know
that he shouldn't have been digging in her den.

Tioga doesn't heed Keisha's displeasure
and goes back to digging.

Keisha decides enough is enough and drags Tioga out of the den by the back fur.

Merlin, the alpha male, looks over the den with his son, Tioga, as Keisha looks on.

Merlin takes a quick look at the den for himself.

CHAPTER 3

When I first started as a volunteer in 2006, the wolves were still reproducing. I recall approximately twenty pups, give or take a few, being born in those early years. Wolf Sanctuary of PA is a rescue facility and does not release, give, or sell any wolves, and so as the packs grew, it became necessary to control the puppy population either by spaying or neutering. This served two purposes: It eliminated the gene pool from becoming too thin in a pack due to inter-pack breeding, and it left space to rescue more wolves. There are times I wish we could have puppies again but understand that we have to rescue as many wolves as we can—and unfortunately, there are many. These photos bring back fond memories.

Wolf Pups

Only days old, Hope (shown in this photo) and her brother, Aries, were pulled from their den because their mother died shortly after they were born.

The last litter born in the Big Pack was comprised of five males, all with names beginning with "*L*"; we call them the L Brothers. Shown here, Lenape, was only a few weeks old.

Born in the Big Pack, Lazarus was brought out of the den by his mother, Lucky, so that he didn't infect the rest of the litter with the upper respiratory infection he had. Taken to the veterinarian for treatment, Lazarus could not be returned to the pack for fear of rejection by its members. He was placed with Aries and Hope, and they became the three-pack.

Lincoln, two months old, is another one of the L Brothers.

Pups learning tactics from Trinity (standing behind Frodo) as he watches on. When the pups are old enough to explore outside the den, they are taken care of by the entire pack. The alphas may choose certain wolves to train the pups. This can include hunting tactics, such as how to apply the throat hold that is used to crush the wind pipe and suffocate their prey, or how to wrap the rear legs with their front legs to trip the animal they're chasing. The pups are taught how to defend themselves as well. Being able to witness and photograph this process was a lifetime experience that I will never forget.

More of the pups as they enjoy their new freedom to walk around within their pack knowing they are surrounded by the protection of the adult wolves.

Lincoln being carried by his mother, Lucky.

Aries, a brother to Hope, a couple of weeks old. Spencer, their mother, passed shortly after they were born. Aries was one of the last pups to be born at Wolf Sanctuary of PA, in December of 2008.

CHAPTER 4

From the first time I heard the wolves howl, it has never grown old. I would practice "my" howl on top of the hill when I was alone. It took about two years before the packs would respond. The first time was the day that we lost Murphy, the alpha male of the Big Pack. Denny and I were down along the creek remembering all the things that Murphy had taught us. I said to Denny, "I'm going to give Murphy a final howl." Much to our surprise, all of the wolves responded by howling back as if they knew what I was doing. The wolf howl is something that everyone should experience in person. If you are fortunate enough to hear it, you won't forget it.

The Wolf's Song

A howling good time is had by all. A wolf's howl is one of its ways to communicate, both within the pack or to other wolf packs. The alpha male will use the howl during a hunt to direct or call in the pack to eat. He may use it to let other packs know they are too close to his pack's territory. A pack may also howl just as a social event.

A wolf that lost his/her mate may use the "lone wolf howl" during its period of mourning or separation anxiety. The male alpha usually is the one to start the howl within the pack. Each wolf's howl is different from the other just like there are no two human voices alike.

Whether it's playing rough, chewing sticks, or just running, the wolves get plenty of exercise…

CHAPTER 5

Wolves love to run and play, especially during the winter when it's nice and cool to them. If you get to witness a play session, you may think that they're trying to kill each other, and sometimes they do receive injuries that may cause a limp for a short time. Typically, it's just rough play and demonstrating their position within the pack.

Exercise and Play

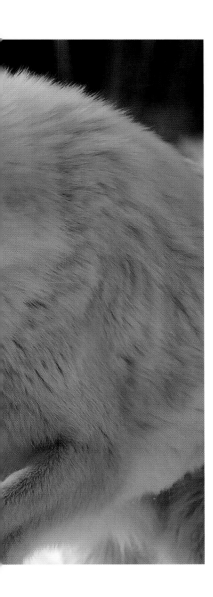

I once read that wolves rest fifty percent of their time by nature so that they always have the strength to endure a strenuous hunt led by their alpha male. They are either napping and keenly aware of what is going on around them or they are in a very deep sleep. When they're in a deep sleep, it's difficult to tell if they are breathing. You have to watch very closely to see any chest movement. Darin tells the story of how he watched Winston, a beta wolf in the Big Pack at one point, for a period of time until he accepted Winston's passing. But when Darin came back with his truck to remove Winston, he found him standing there looking at him as if to say, "Who died?" Thor, a blind wolf at the Sanctuary, has also played the "deep sleep" trick on us.

Wolves, no matter what color they are, are excellent at camouflaging themselves. One sunny winter day I was out taking a head count and looked for Thor throughout his territory for over one hour. Not finding any sign of him, I thought the worst—since he was fifteen years old at the time. Then, I saw a glimmer of silver behind a log and there he was sunning himself, not a care in the world. Wolves really know how to toy with our human emotions.

Rest and Relaxation

A wolf's fur has two layers. An insulating layer that is so dense, they don't lose body heat and an outer layer called "guard hairs" that protects them from the elements.

By nature, wolves rest or relax up to fifty percent of their time. This is so that if the alpha male chooses them to go on a hunt, they are rested and ready for the task.

CHAPTER 7

I sometimes use the phrase "wolves sleep with their eyes open." Even if they are lying with their head on the ground and eyes closed, they appear acutely aware of everything around them. They can be on their feet and investigating something in an instant.

Always Alert

Extremely curious and aware of their surroundings, wolves use body language to express themselves. It can be a gentle stare or an intense one, or a baring of the teeth along with a growl and flattened ears.

CHAPTER 8

The hierarchy the wolf pack lives within is evident but is especially displayed during a feeding event. For example, it's an education to watch a wolf pack eating a deer. The alpha male usually eats first, devouring as much as his stomach will hold. He typically will eat the high protein parts first. Sometimes wolves will bury meat for a later meal. On numerous occasions, I've watched them eat so much that they can barely sit or lie down without discomfort. When the alpha male is finished, which sometimes can take hours or even days, the rest of the pack will eat. At times, I've observed the elders of the Big Pack attempting to sneak in on the younger males to get meat, but they are usually chased away. During earlier years, when Murphy was the alpha of the Big Pack and his brother Winston was the beta, it was not uncommon for the two of them to keep the entire pack of sixteen wolves at a distance while they ate. They would take turns lunging at would-be aggressors trying to get a small piece of meat.

Eating Habits

The alpha male eats first and isn't afraid to exhibit his authority towards any other wolf that attempts to eat without his permission.

Merlin, an alpha male, had just finished eating what Darin estimated to be about twenty pounds of deer. His belly couldn't hold any more. The mud on his nose indicates that he buried more meat for later on. He then went on the offensive and kept the other members of the pack at bay, even though he couldn't possibly eat another bite. The others got to eat, but not until he was ready to let them.

A prized deer leg bone is buried for later.

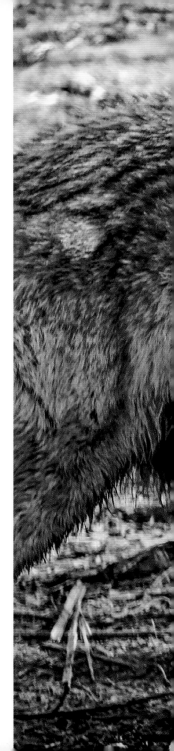

Smokey, on the left, is letting her daughter, Solo, know that it's not her turn to eat just yet. Smokey was fifteen years old at the time, but had no trouble holding her own as the female alpha in the pack.

Unlike humans, wolves are able to use snow as a water source without losing any body heat.

CHAPTER 9

Winter is my favorite time to photograph the wolves. They have their winter fur and are more active. The wolves love the snow and it appears the colder the better. The sanctuary is required to have an enclosure of some type in every pack area. Interestingly enough, the wolves don't use them for protection from weather. As a matter of fact, they rarely use them for anything. Wolves are equipped for the outdoors with thick fur, and have additional fur between their toes and in their ears that helps protect them from the cold. They also have more blood vessels in their paw pads to keep them from freezing. Research tells us that a wolf can function in temperatures that reach 25 to 30 degrees Fahrenheit below freezing. They love to play and run in the snow or move ever so quietly through their area as they take a winter walk.

Winter Walks

Taking photos of wolves in the snow is a rewarding experience. Perseverance is a must.

A few of my favorite photos…

CHAPTER 10

Favorites

Jake has become a favorite of everyone and has been adopted many times. I'm still trying to figure out why "she" is named Jake. When I took this photo, she was stalking and attacking flies that were landing on a nearby piece of meat. She was not happy about it.

Lucas always knows you are there whether he is looking at you or not. There is no sneaking up on a wolf. They can hear for approximately twelve miles and can smell four to five miles depending on conditions. It's fun to think that you have snuck up on one, only to realize that you haven't when they turn and give you that penetrating stare.

Merlin receiving a nuzzle from his son, Tioga.

Tayha is as elusive as they come.

Billy was one of the first wolves I photographed. This photo was
posted in the *National Geographic Online Magazine* photo library.

Smokey was the matriarch of Wolf Sanctuary of PA. She was the mother or grandmother of every wolf in the Big Pack and mothered her second pack known as Smokey's Pack.

Mika and Spirit during a heavy snow.

Merlin's mournful eyes express the sadness and separation anxiety he felt after losing Keisha, the alpha female, the day before. His son, Tioga, tried his best to comfort his father without visible success. He was never the same and passed ten months later. He was truly an educator to wolf and humans alike.

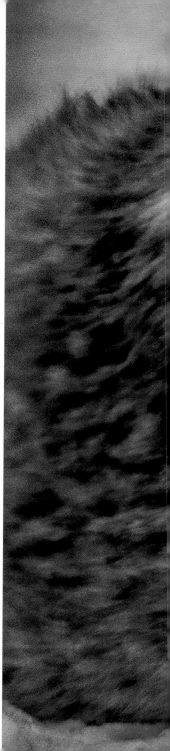

Thor is gorgeous to photograph in color or black and white.

It's almost as if Bear likes to pose for pictures.

Conclusion

I've been afforded the rare opportunity to study and photograph wolves, a part of North American history. The knowledge that I've gained from this experience, both in life and as a photographer, is priceless and cannot be taught in a classroom alone. When wolves were reintroduced into Yellowstone National Park, a positive ecological impact was realized after the first year. I find it difficult to understand why people, the only predator to the wolf, are willing to bring this magnificent creature to an endangered species or even worse, extinction. You can help by donating to Wolf Sanctuary of PA. Visit the website at www.wolfsanctuarypa.org to learn more.

—Chuck Rineer

Bibliography

Busch, Robert H. 2007. *New and Revised. The Wolf Almanac: A Celebration of Wolves and Their World*. Guilford, CT: The Lyons Press, An Imprint of the Globe Pequot Press.

Mancini, Michelle. "Ecological, Social, and Political Impact of Wolf Reintroduction to Yellowstone National Park, Wyoming." (Master's thesis, University of Pennsylvania), YouTube video, 1:41:22, posted by Michelle Mancini, August 2015, http://www.youtube.com.

Savage, Candace Sherk. 1949, *Wolves*. Vancouver, British Columbia, Canada: Douglas & McIntyre Ltd.

Wolf Sanctuary of PA. www.wolfsanctuarypa.org.

As the moon will light
many paths in your life,
acknowledge the wisdom
of the wolf and it will
lead you down the paths
of experience.

- Chuck Rineer

I took pictures of the Super Moon during
a photo shoot in the Outer Banks of
North Carolina in November 2016 and
created the composite utilizing a photo
of Little Girl doing her thing!